Alfred's Basic Piano Library

Piano

Ear Training Book
Complete Level 1

FOR THE LATER BEGINNER

Gayle Kowalchyk ◆ E. L. Lancaster

Second Edition
Copyright © MCMXCVI by Alfred Publishing Co., Inc.

Instructions for Use

1. This EAR TRAINING BOOK is designed to be used with Alfred's Basic Piano Library, COMPLETE LEVEL 1 Lesson Book.

2. This book is coordinated page-by-page with the LESSON BOOK, and assignments are ideally made according to the instructions in the upper right corner of each page of the EAR TRAINING BOOK.

3. Many students enjoy completing these pages so much that they will want to go beyond the assigned material. However, it is best to wait until the indicated pages in the LESSON BOOK have been covered before the corresponding material in this book is studied.

4. This EAR TRAINING BOOK reinforces each concept presented in the LESSON BOOK and specifically focuses on the training and development of the ear. Rhythmic, melodic and intervallic concepts are drilled throughout the book to provide the necessary systematic reinforcement for the student.

5. Each page is designed to be completed using approximately five minutes of the lesson time. Examples for each page are given for the teacher (pages 52–64).

Low Sounds and High Sounds

1. Your teacher will play LOW and HIGH sounds.
   - Circle LOW if you hear LOW sounds.
   - Circle HIGH if you hear HIGH sounds.
2. Your teacher will play sounds that go UP or DOWN.
   - Circle the arrow POINTING UP if the sounds go UP.
   - Circle the arrow POINTING DOWN if the sounds go DOWN.

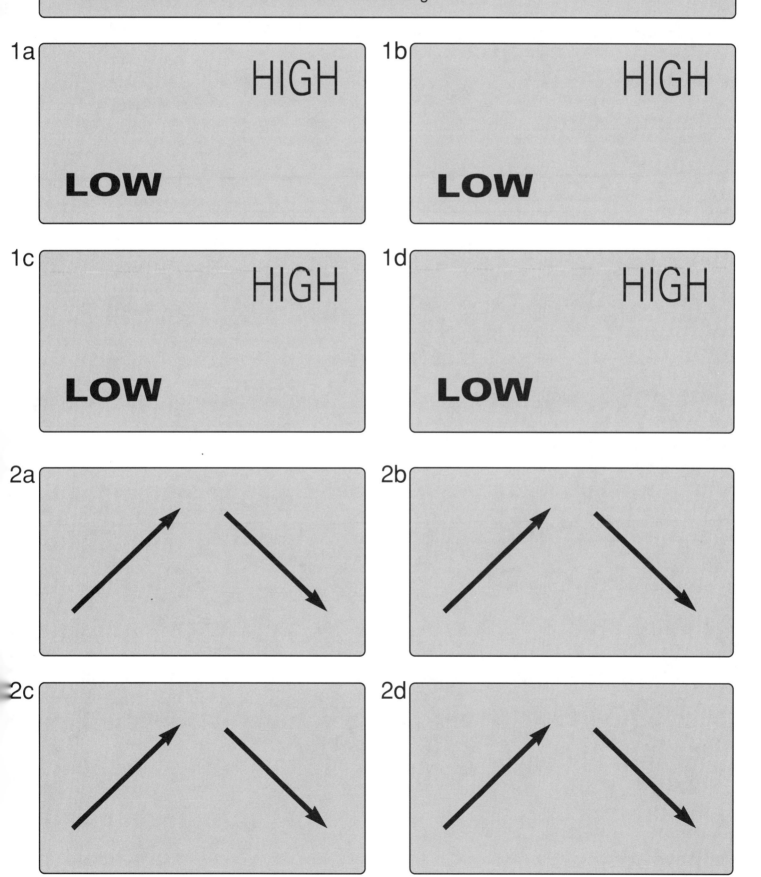

TEACHER: See page 52.

Use with page 5.

Quarter Note and Half Note

1. Your teacher will clap a rhythm pattern. Circle the pattern that you hear.
2. Your teacher will clap a rhythm pattern using QUARTER and HALF notes.
   Draw the missing note (♩ or 𝅗𝅥) in the box.

1a
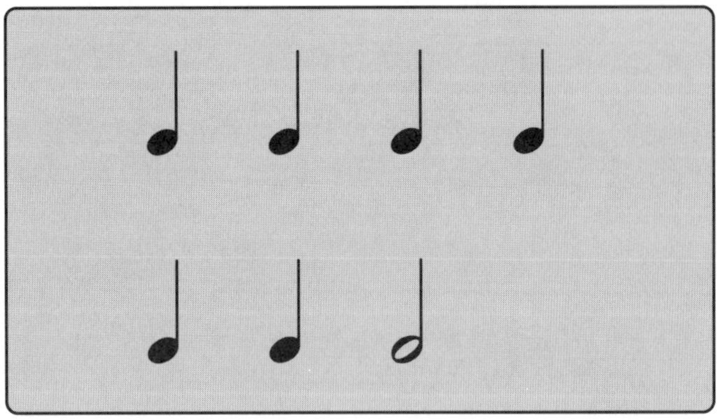

1b
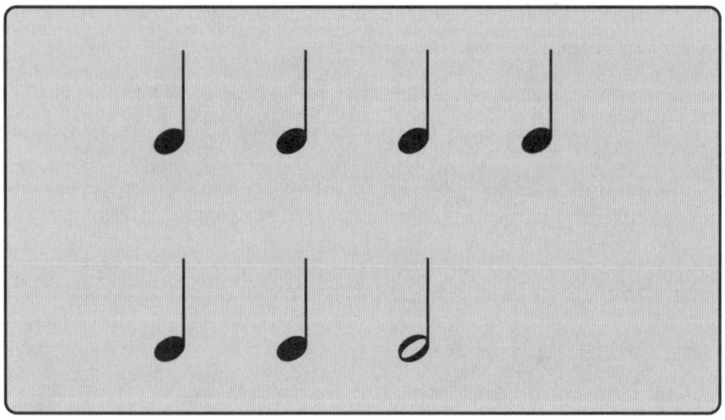

1c
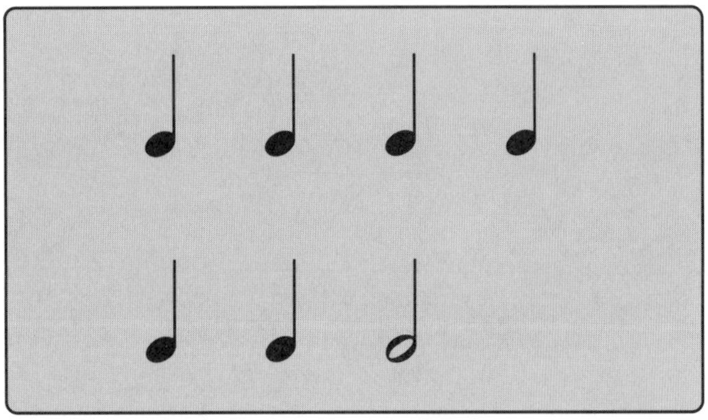

1d
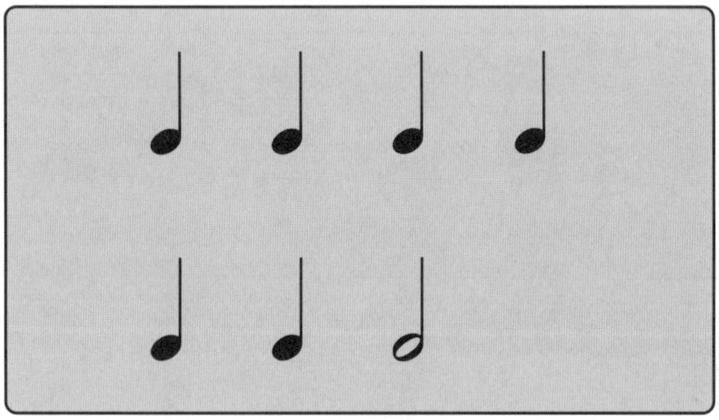

2a
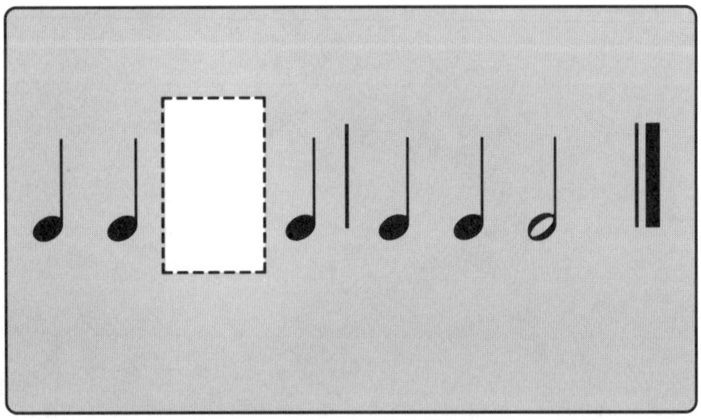

2b
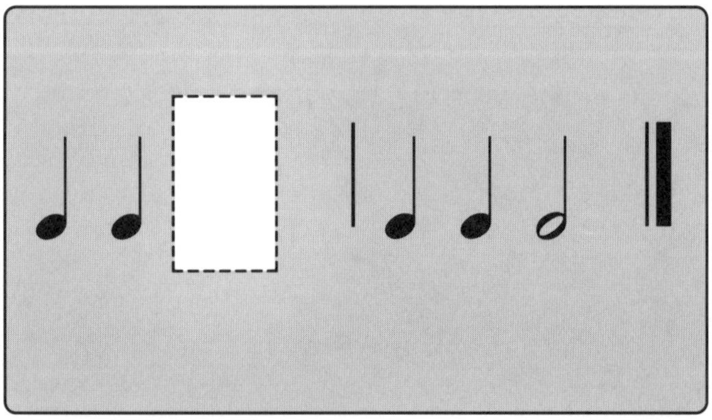

2c
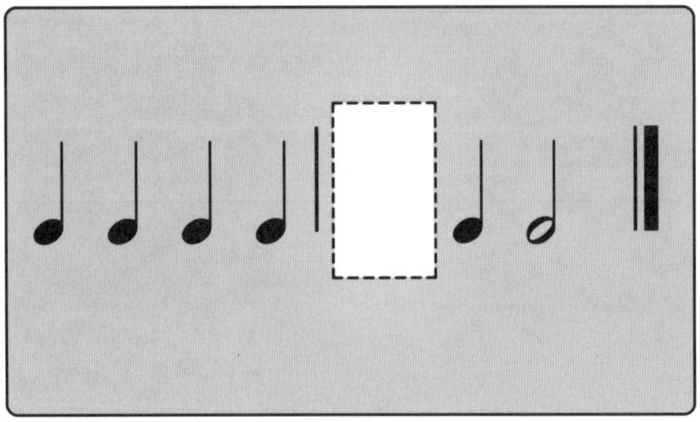

2d
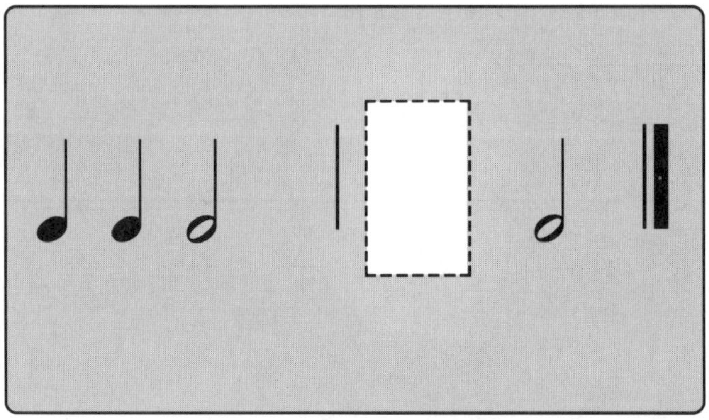

TEACHER: See page 52.

Quarter, Half and Whole Notes

1. Your teacher will clap a rhythm pattern. Circle the pattern that you hear.

2. Your teacher will clap a rhythm pattern using QUARTER, HALF and WHOLE notes.
   Draw the missing note (♩ or ♪ or o) in the box.

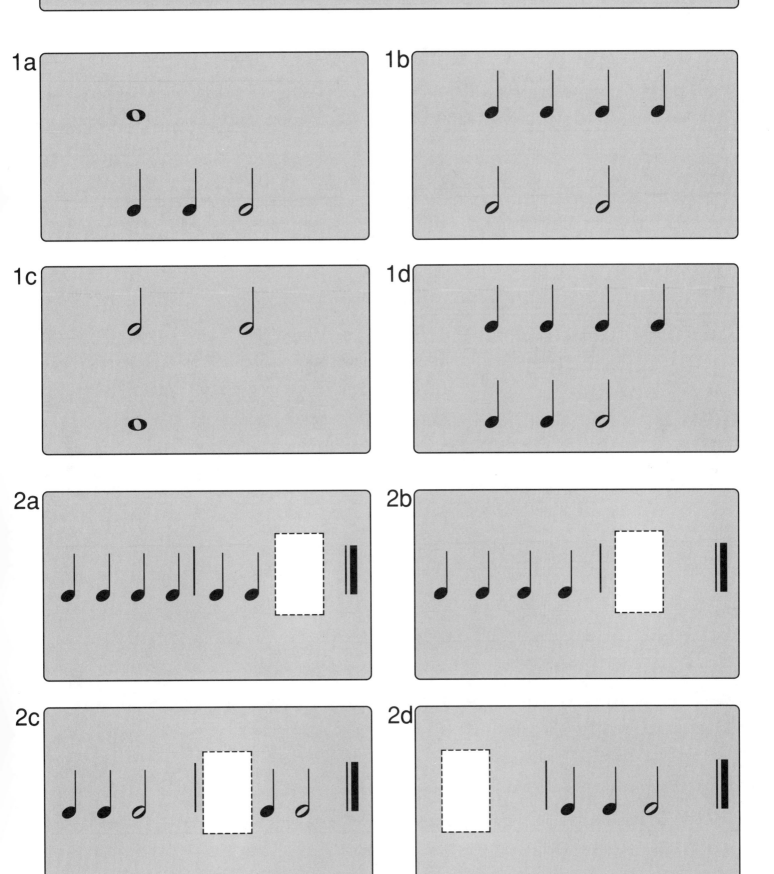

Use with page 7.

Rhythm Patterns

1. Your teacher will clap two rhythm patterns.
   - Circle SAME if the patterns are the SAME.
   - Circle DIFFERENT if the patterns are DIFFERENT.
2. Your teacher will clap one of the rhythm patterns. Write the pattern that you hear.

1a   SAME   *DIFFERENT*

1b   SAME   *DIFFERENT*

1c   SAME   *DIFFERENT*

1d   SAME   *DIFFERENT*

2a

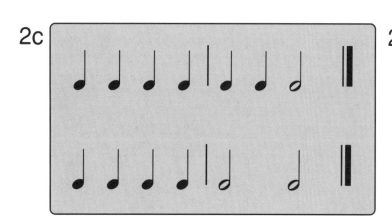

Pattern:_____

2b

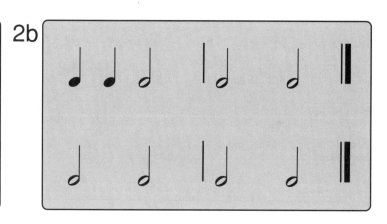

Pattern:_____

2c

Pattern:_____

2d

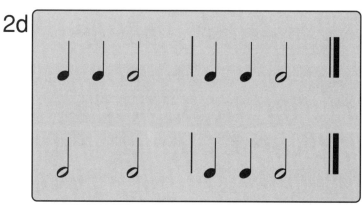

Pattern:_____

Musical Alphabet

Your teacher will play the letters of the MUSICAL ALPHABET going UP or DOWN.

• Circle the letters GOING UP if the alphabet goes UP.

• Circle the letters GOING DOWN if the alphabet goes DOWN.

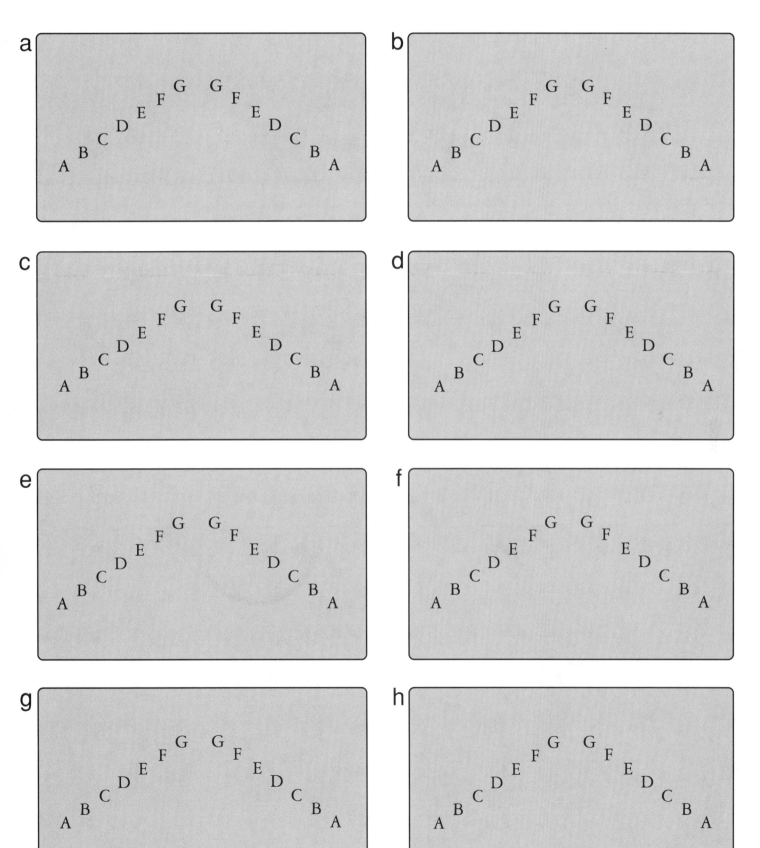

Use with page 10.

Middle C Position

Your teacher will play patterns that go UP or DOWN in the MIDDLE C POSITION.
Circle the pattern that you hear.

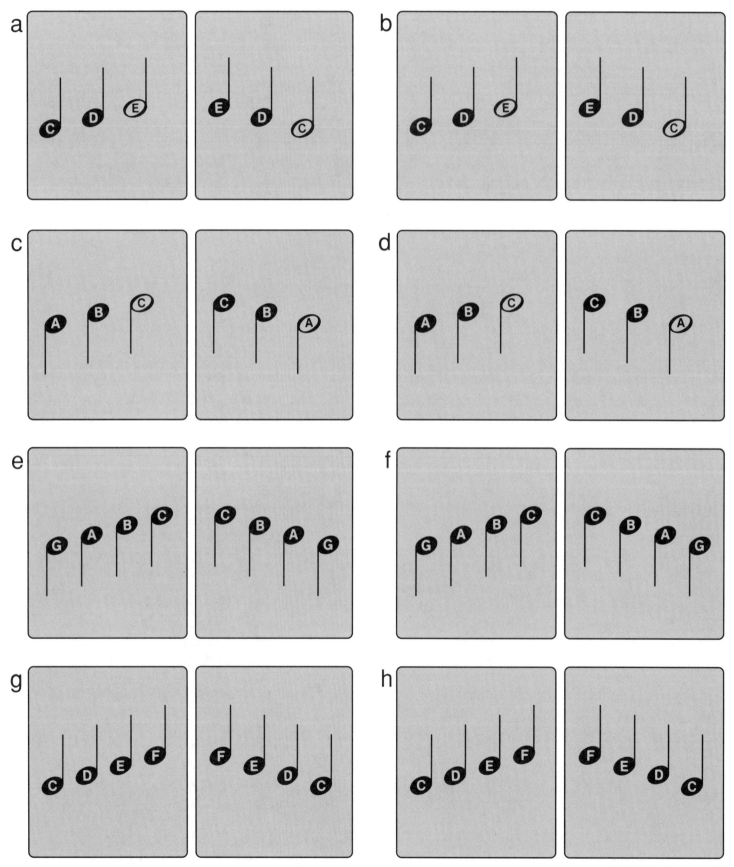

TEACHER: See page 53.

Use with page 13.

Bass Clef

1. Your teacher will play REPEATED notes or notes STEPPING DOWN.
   Circle the pattern that you hear.

2. Your teacher will play REPEATED notes or notes STEPPING UP.
   Circle the pattern that you hear.

1a

1b

1c

1d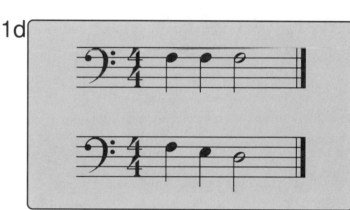

2a

2b

2c

2d

TEACHER: See page 54.

Use with page 15.

Treble Clef

1. Your teacher will play REPEATED notes or notes STEPPING DOWN.
   Circle the pattern that you hear.

2. Your teacher will play REPEATED notes or notes STEPPING UP.
   Circle the pattern that you hear.

1a

1b

1c

1d

2a

2b

2c

2d

TEACHER: See page 54.

Melodic Patterns

1. Your teacher will play patterns that go UP or DOWN in the C POSITION.
   Circle the pattern that you hear.

2. Your teacher will play melodies in the C POSITION.
   Draw the missing note in the box.

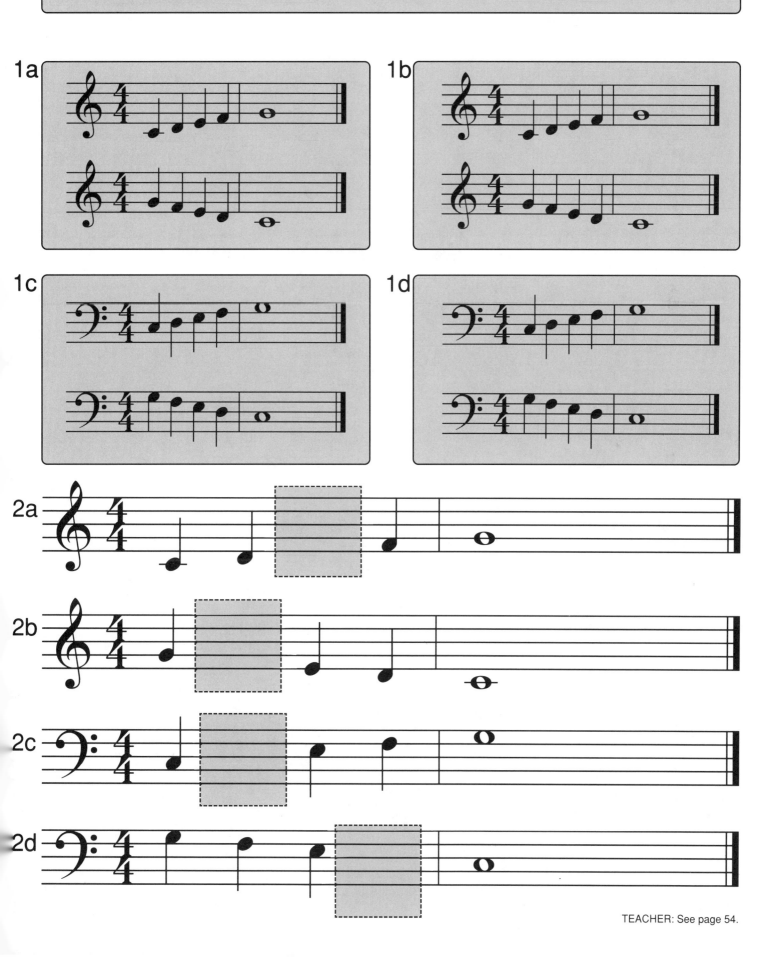

12

Use with page 18.

2nds

1. Your teacher will play 2nds that move UP or DOWN. Circle the example that you hear.
2. Your teacher will play 2nds ABOVE or BELOW the given note.
   Draw the second note and write the name of both notes on the lines below the staff.

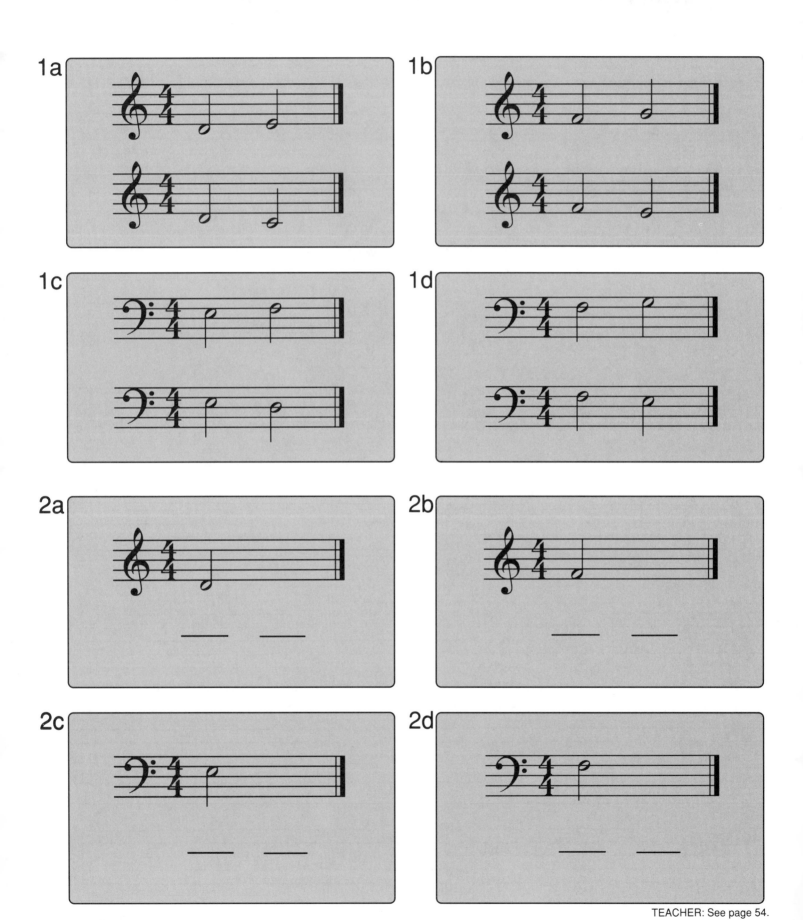

Quarter, Half and Dotted Half Notes

1. Your teacher will clap a rhythm pattern.
   Circle the pattern that you hear.
2. Your teacher will clap a rhythm pattern.
   Write the time signature and the pattern that you hear.

1a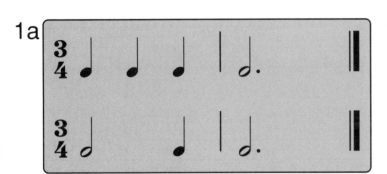

1b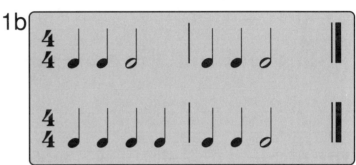

1c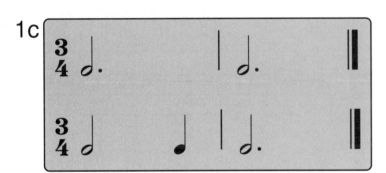

1d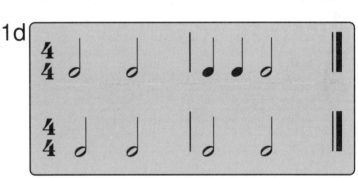

2a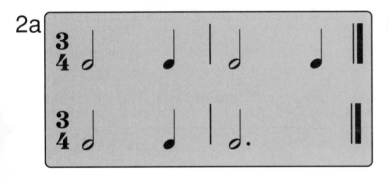

2b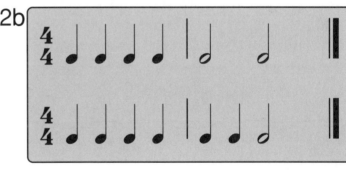

Pattern:_____ Pattern:_____

2c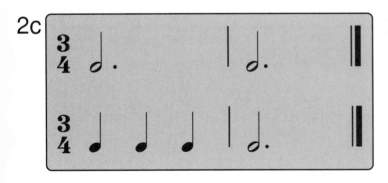

2d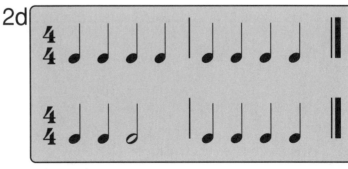

Pattern:_____ Pattern:_____

TEACHER: See page 55.

Use with page 20.

Legato, Piano and Forte

1. Your teacher will play four melodies.
   Draw a SLUR to connect the first and last note of each melody if it is played LEGATO.

2. Your teacher will play SOFT and LOUD sounds.
   - Circle the *p* if you hear SOFT sounds.
   - Circle the *f* if you hear LOUD sounds.

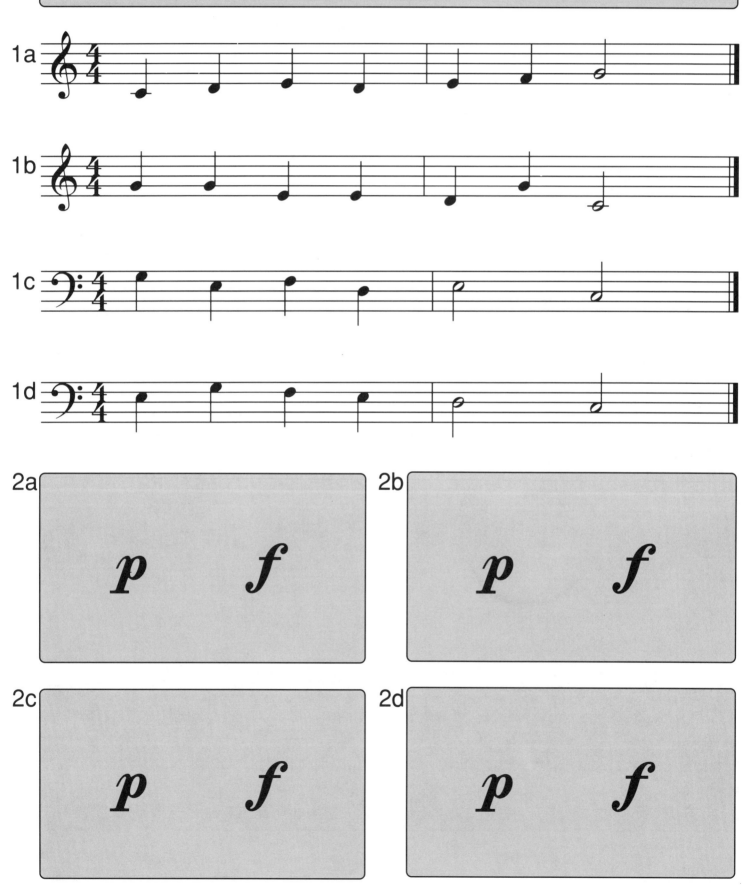

TEACHER: See page 55.

Tied Notes

1. Your teacher will play TIED NOTES or a SLUR.
   Circle the example that you hear.
2. Your teacher will clap a rhythm pattern.
   Add a curved line for each tie that you hear.

1a

1b

1c

1d

2a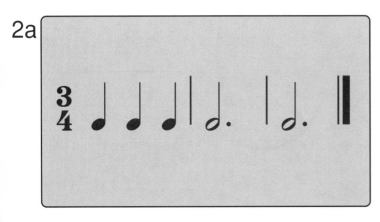

2b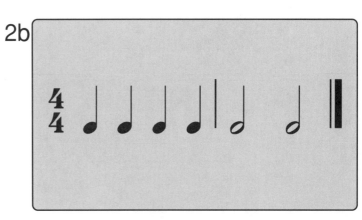

2c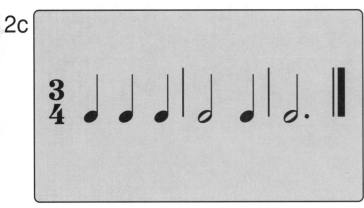

2d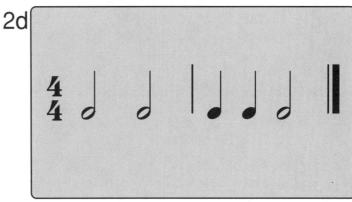

TEACHER: See page 55.

Use with page 22.

3rds

1. Your teacher will play 3rds that move UP or DOWN.
   Circle the example that you hear.

2. Your teacher will play 3rds ABOVE or BELOW the given note.
   Draw the second note and write the name of both notes on the lines below the staff.

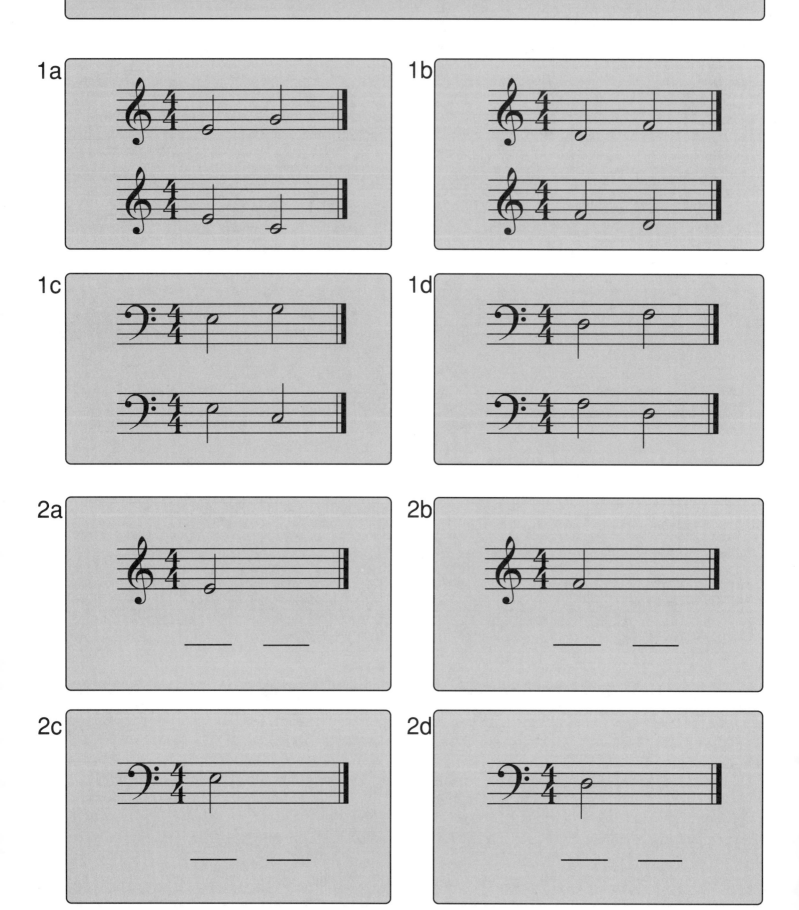

Rhythm Patterns

1. Your teacher will clap two rhythm patterns.
   - Circle SAME if the patterns are the SAME.
   - Circle DIFFERENT if the patterns are DIFFERENT.
2. Your teacher will clap a rhythm pattern. Circle the pattern that you hear.

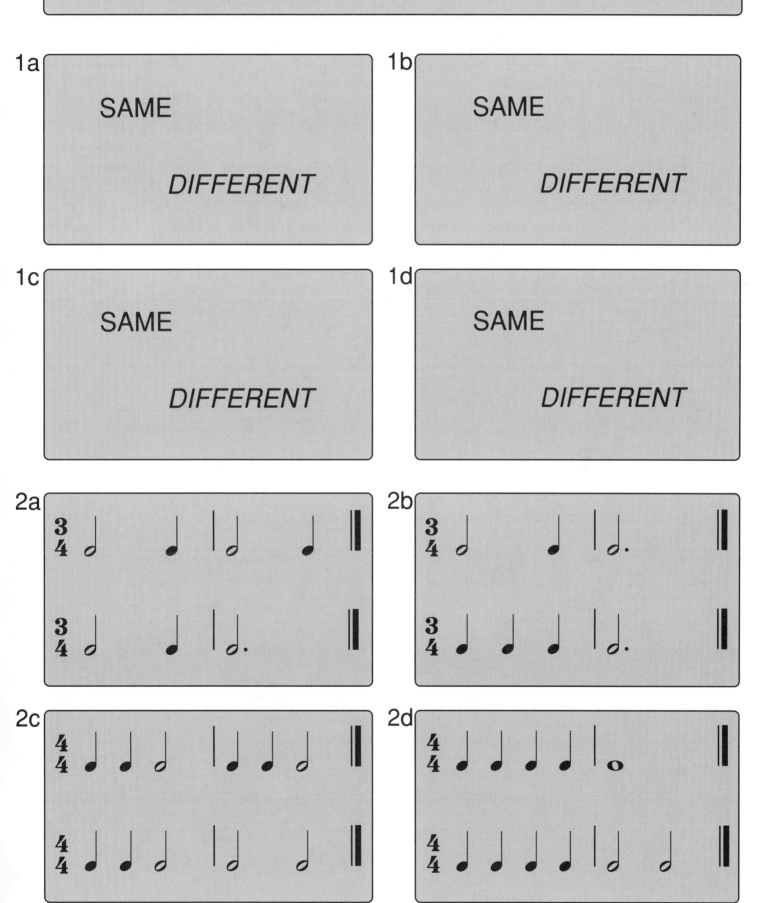

TEACHER: See page 56.

Use with page 24.

Melodic and Harmonic Intervals

Your teacher will play MELODIC or HARMONIC 2nds or 3rds.

• Circle the example that you hear.

• Write M if it is MELODIC or H if it is HARMONIC along with the interval number (2 or 3) on the line.
  Example: M2

a

b

c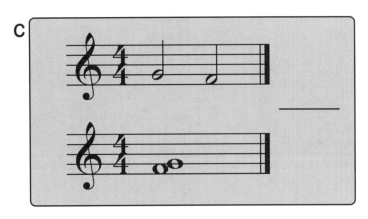

d

e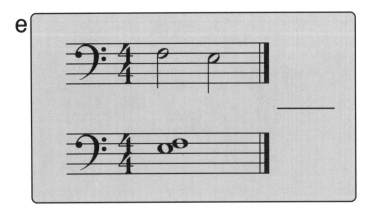

f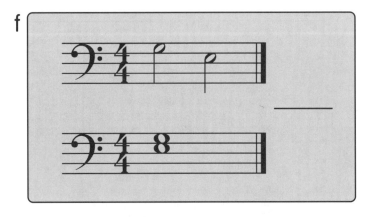

g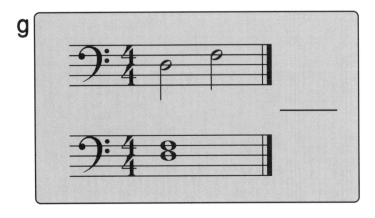

h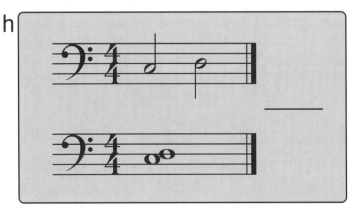

TEACHER: See page 56.

Use with page 25.

Quarter Rest

1. Your teacher will clap a rhythm pattern.
   Draw the missing QUARTER NOTE (♩) or QUARTER REST (𝄽) in the box.
2. Your teacher will clap rhythm patterns using QUARTER, HALF and DOTTED HALF NOTES.
   • Fill in each QUARTER NOTE that you hear.
   • Add a dot to each DOTTED HALF NOTE that you hear.

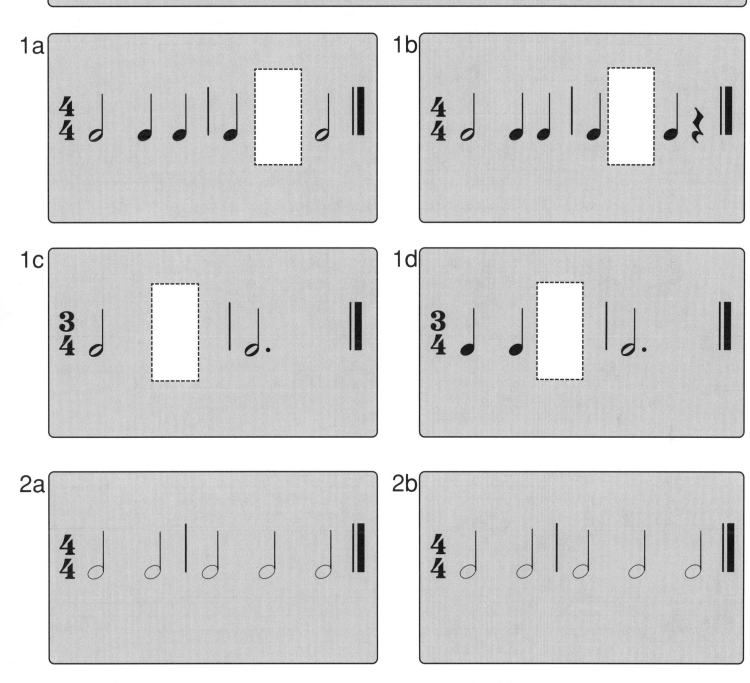

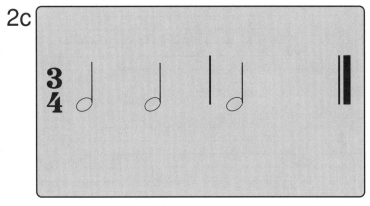

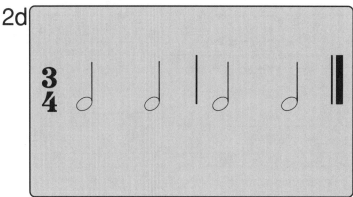

TEACHER: See page 56.

Use with page 27.

Melodic Patterns

1. Your teacher will play patterns that go UP or DOWN in the C POSITION.
   Circle the pattern that you hear.

2. Your teacher will play melodies in the C POSITION.
   Draw the missing note in the box.

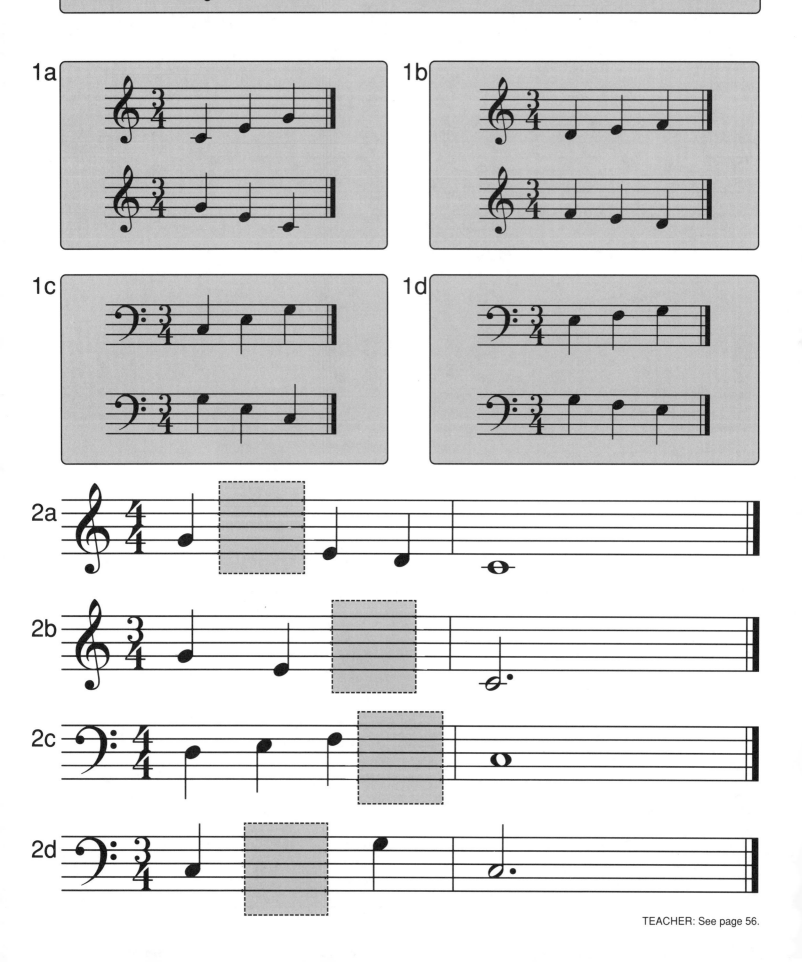

4ths

1. Your teacher will play 4ths that move UP or DOWN.
   Circle the example that you hear.
2. Your teacher will play intervals of a 2nd or 4th.
   Circle the interval that you hear.

1a

1b

1c

1d

2a

2b

2c

2d

TEACHER: See page 57.

Use with page 29.

Whole Rest

1. Your teacher will clap a rhythm pattern.
   Draw the missing WHOLE NOTE (o) or WHOLE REST (▬) in the box.
2. Your teacher will clap a rhythm pattern.
   Draw the missing notes in the third measure using ♩ ♩ and ♩.

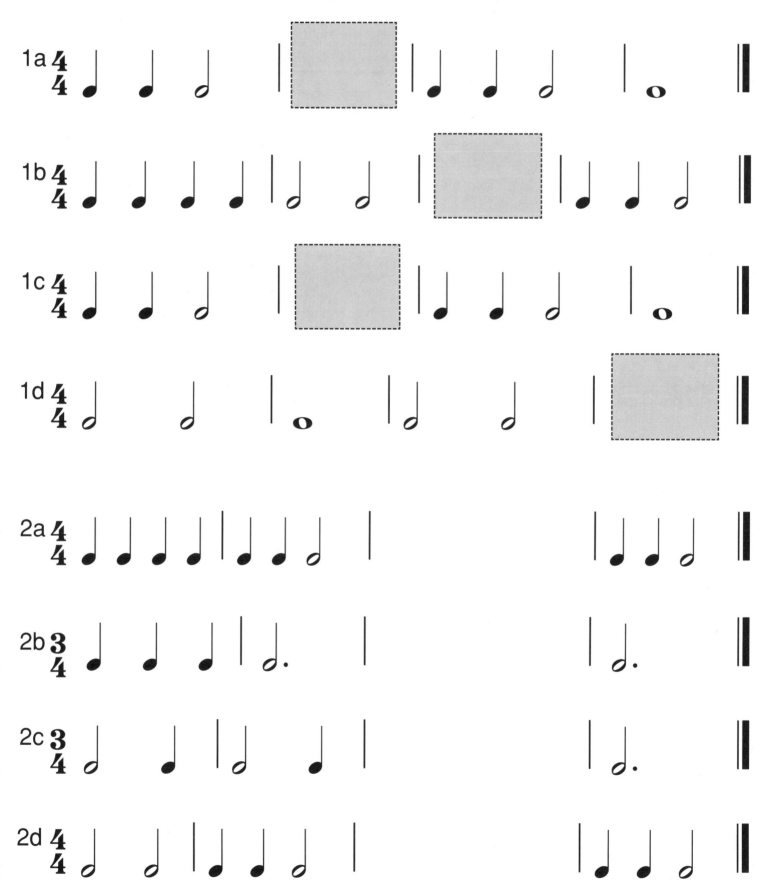

5ths

1. Your teacher will play 5ths that move UP or DOWN.
   Circle the example that you hear.
2. Your teacher will play intervals of a 3rd or 5th.
   Circle the interval that you hear.

1a

1b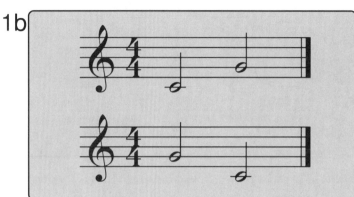

1c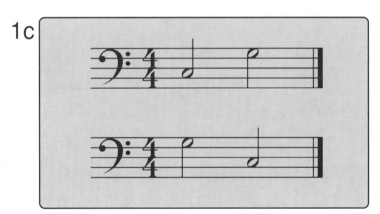

1d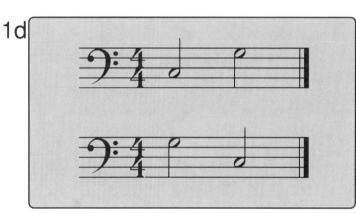

2a

2b

2c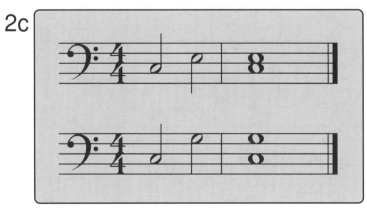

2d

Use with page 32.

G Position

1. Your teacher will play patterns that go UP or DOWN in the G POSITION.
   Circle the pattern that you hear.
2. Your teacher will play melodies in the G POSITION.
   Draw the missing note in the box.

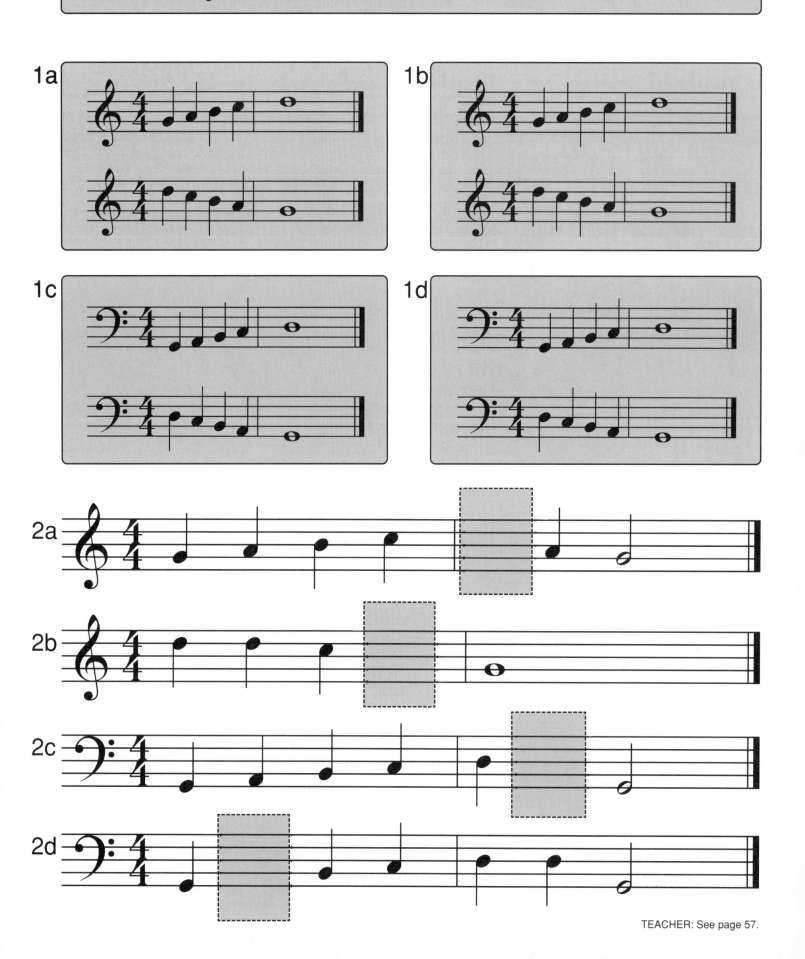

Half Rest

1. Your teacher will clap a rhythm pattern.
   Draw the missing notes and rests in the second measure using ♩ ♩ ♩. 𝄾 and ▬

2. Your teacher will play MELODIC or HARMONIC 4ths or 5ths.
   • Circle the example that you hear.
   • Write M if it is MELODIC or H if it is HARMONIC along with the interval number (4 or 5) on the line.

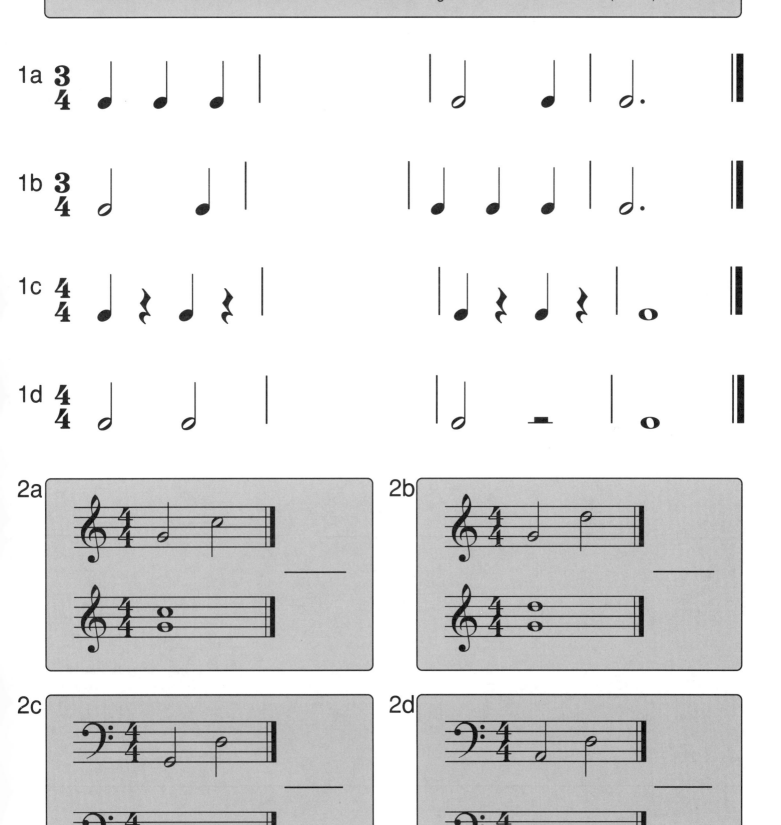

Use with page 35.

Crescendo and Diminuendo

1. Your teacher will play four melodies.
   • Add a CRESCENDO sign (<) UNDER the staff if the melody gets GRADUALLY LOUDER.
   • Add a DIMINUENDO sign (>) UNDER the staff if the melody gets GRADUALLY SOFTER.
2. Your teacher will play melodies that CRESCENDO or DIMINUENDO.
   • Circle the CRESCENDO sign if the melody gets GRADUALLY LOUDER.
   • Circle the DIMINUENDO sign if the melody gets GRADUALLY SOFTER.

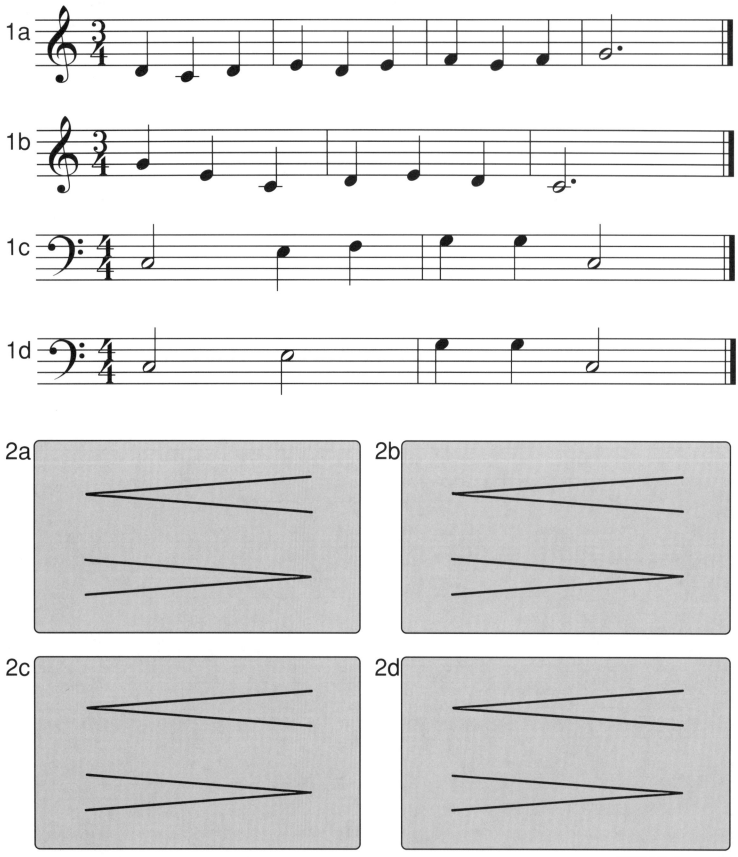

TEACHER: See page 58.

Sharp

1. Your teacher will play two notes.
   If the second note is the next key to the RIGHT (up), draw a SHARP (♯) in front of it.
2. Your teacher will play patterns in G POSITION.
   Circle the pattern that you hear.

1a

1b

1c

1d
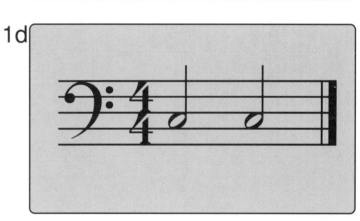

2a

2b

2c

2d

TEACHER: See page 58.

Use with page 38.

Flat

1. Your teacher will play two notes.
   If the second note is the next key to the LEFT (down), draw a FLAT (♭) in front of it.
2. Your teacher will play four melodies. Each melody contains one note with a FLAT.
   Draw a FLAT SIGN before this note.

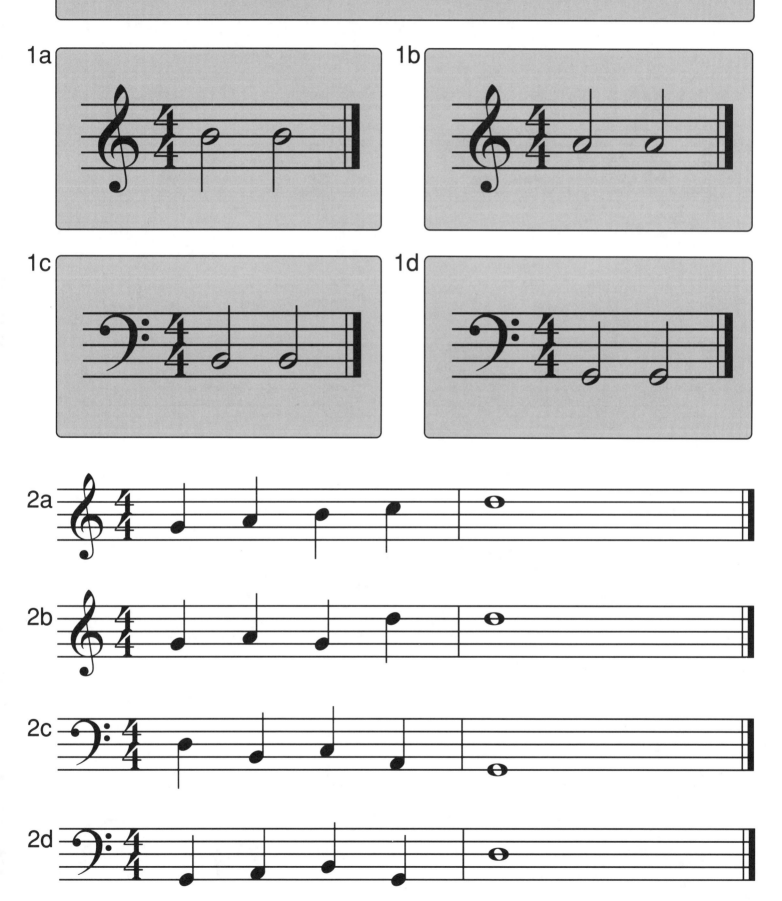

TEACHER: See page 59.

Accent Sign

1. Your teacher will play four melodies. Each melody contains one ACCENT.

   Add an ACCENT SIGN under (𝅘𝅥) or over (𝅘𝅥) the note that is played LOUDER.

2. Your teacher will play four melodies.

   Add a STACCATO DOT under (𝅘𝅥) or over (𝅘𝅥) each note that is played staccato.

Use with page 40.

Staccato

1. Your teacher will play STACCATO and LEGATO melodies.
   • Circle the S if the melody is STACCATO.
   • Circle the L if the melody is LEGATO.
2. Your teacher will play four melodies. Add a STACCATO DOT to each staccato note.
   • If the note stem points DOWN, put the dot OVER the note.
   • If the stem points UP, put the dot UNDER the note.

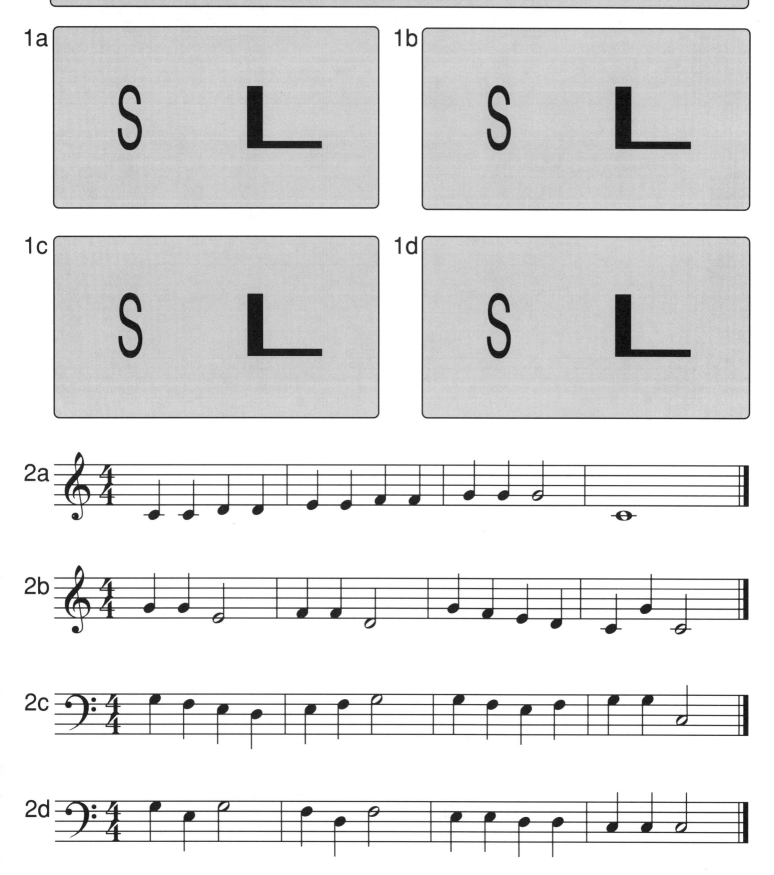

Middle C Position

1. Your teacher will play melodies in the MIDDLE C POSITION.
   Draw the missing note in the box.
2. Your teacher will play melodies in the MIDDLE C POSITION.
   Circle the melody that you hear.

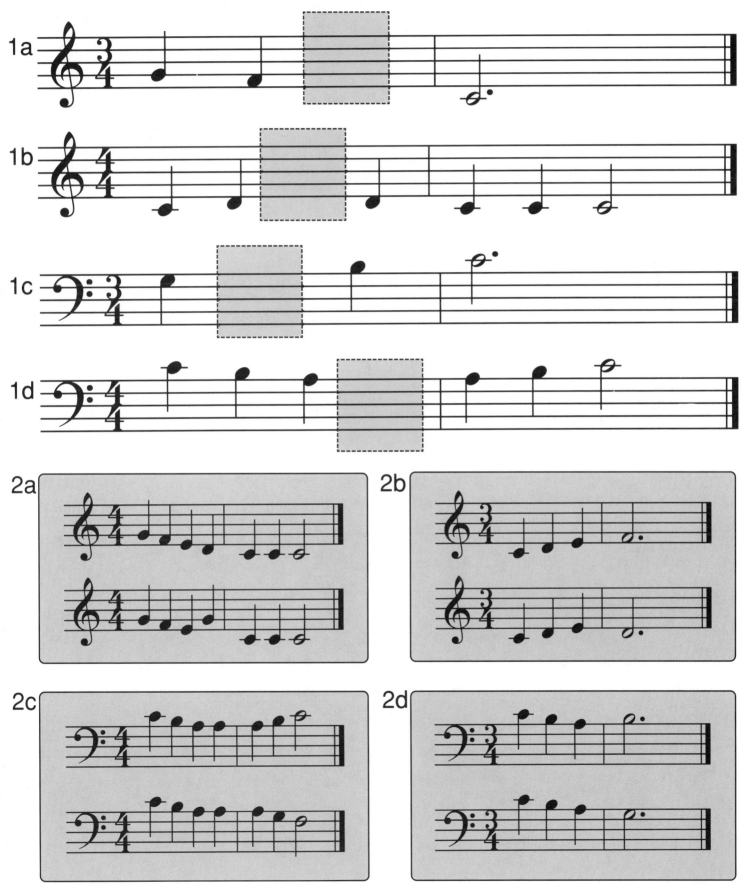

TEACHER: See page 59.

Use with page 43.

Tempo Marks

1. Your teacher will play ALLEGRO and MODERATO melodies.
   - Circle ALLEGRO if the melody is played QUICKLY, HAPPILY.
   - Circle MODERATO if the melody is played MODERATELY.

2. Your teacher will play melodies in $\frac{3}{4}$ or $\frac{4}{4}$ time.

   - Circle the $\frac{3}{4}$ if you hear 3 beats in each measure.

   - Circle the $\frac{4}{4}$ if you hear 4 beats in each measure.

1a

Allegro

Moderato

1b

Allegro

Moderato

1c

Allegro

Moderato

1d

Allegro

Moderato

2a

$\frac{3}{4}$ $\frac{4}{4}$

2b

$\frac{3}{4}$ $\frac{4}{4}$

2c

$\frac{3}{4}$ $\frac{4}{4}$

2d

$\frac{3}{4}$ $\frac{4}{4}$

Rhythm Patterns

1. Your teacher will clap a rhythm pattern.
   Draw the notes in the missing second measure using ♩ ♩ ♩. and 𝅝

2. Your teacher will play melodies that CRESCENDO or DIMINUENDO.
   • Circle the CRESCENDO sign if the melody gets GRADUALLY LOUDER.
   • Circle the DIMINUENDO sign if the melody gets GRADUALLY SOFTER.

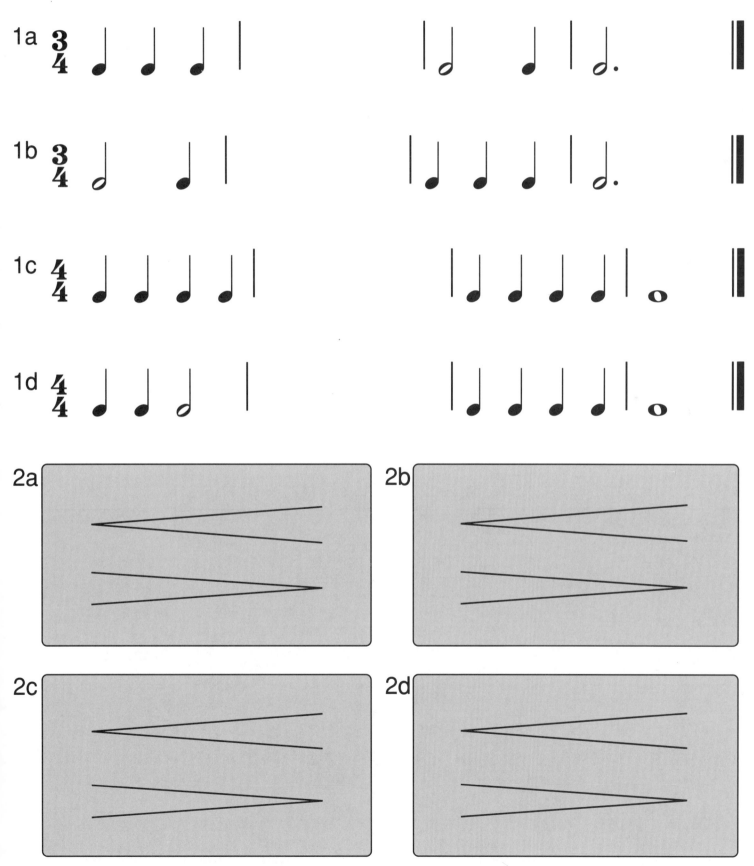

Fermata

1. Your teacher will play four melodies. Each melody contains one FERMATA.
   Add a FERMATA (⌢) over the note that is held longer than its value.
2. Your teacher will play ANDANTE and ADAGIO melodies.
   • Circle ANDANTE if the melody is played MOVING ALONG.
   • Circle ADAGIO if the melody is played SLOWLY.

2a

Andante

Adagio

2b

Andante

Adagio

2c

Andante

Adagio

2d

Andante

Adagio

TEACHER: See page 60.

Eighth Notes

1. Your teacher will clap a rhythm pattern.
   Draw the missing note(s) in the box using ♩ or ♫
2. Your teacher will clap a rhythm pattern.
   Draw the missing notes in the third measure using ♩ ♫ ♩ ♩. and 𝅝

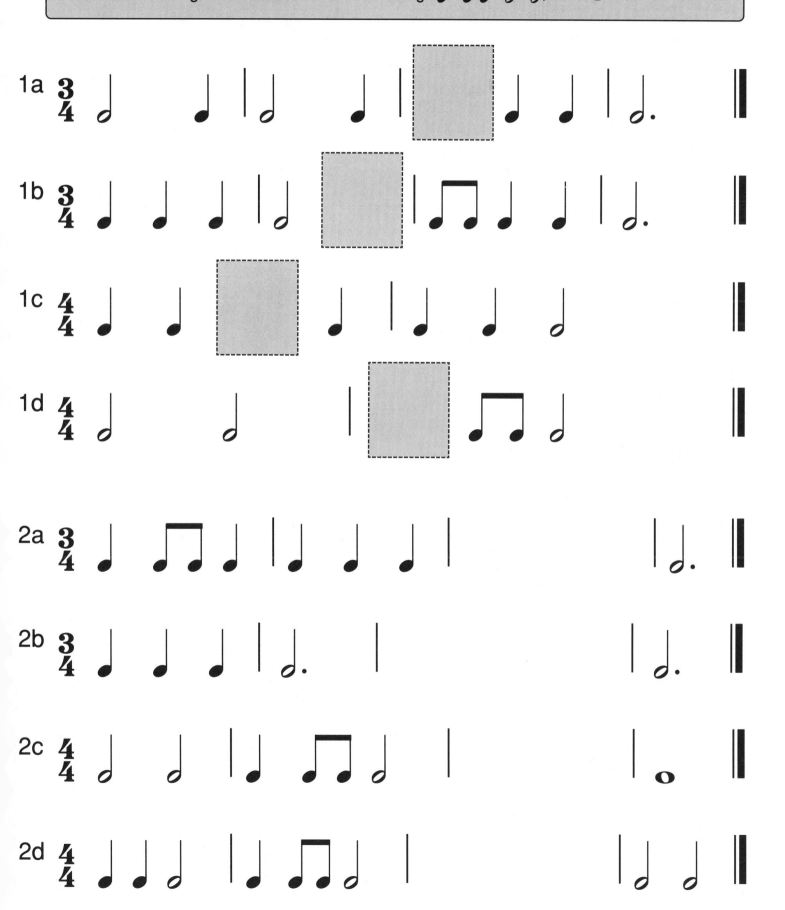

Use with page 48.

Time Signatures

1. Your teacher will play melodies in $\frac{2}{4}$ or $\frac{3}{4}$ time.

   • Circle the $\frac{2}{4}$ if you hear 2 beats in each measure.

   • Circle the $\frac{3}{4}$ if you hear 3 beats in each measure.

2. Your teacher will play melodies in MIDDLE C POSITION. Circle the melody that you hear.

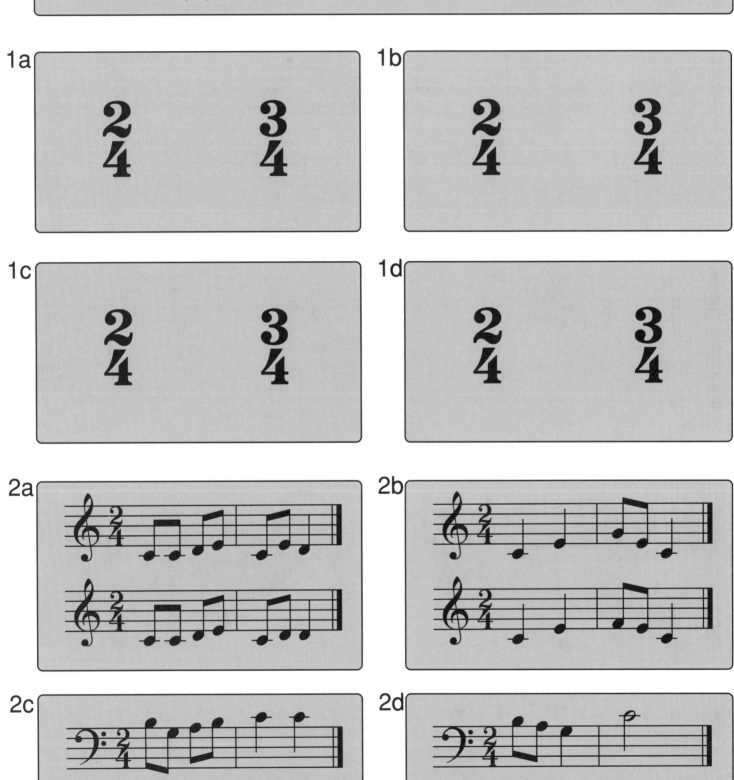

TEACHER: See page 61.

Ritardando

1. Your teacher will play four melodies. Each melody contains a RITARDANDO. Add the RITARDANDO (rit.) below the staff when the tempo begins to GRADUALLY SLOW DOWN.
2. Your teacher will play SOFT or MODERATELY LOUD sounds.
   - Circle the *p* if you hear SOFT sounds.
   - Circle the *mf* if you hear MODERATELY LOUD sounds.

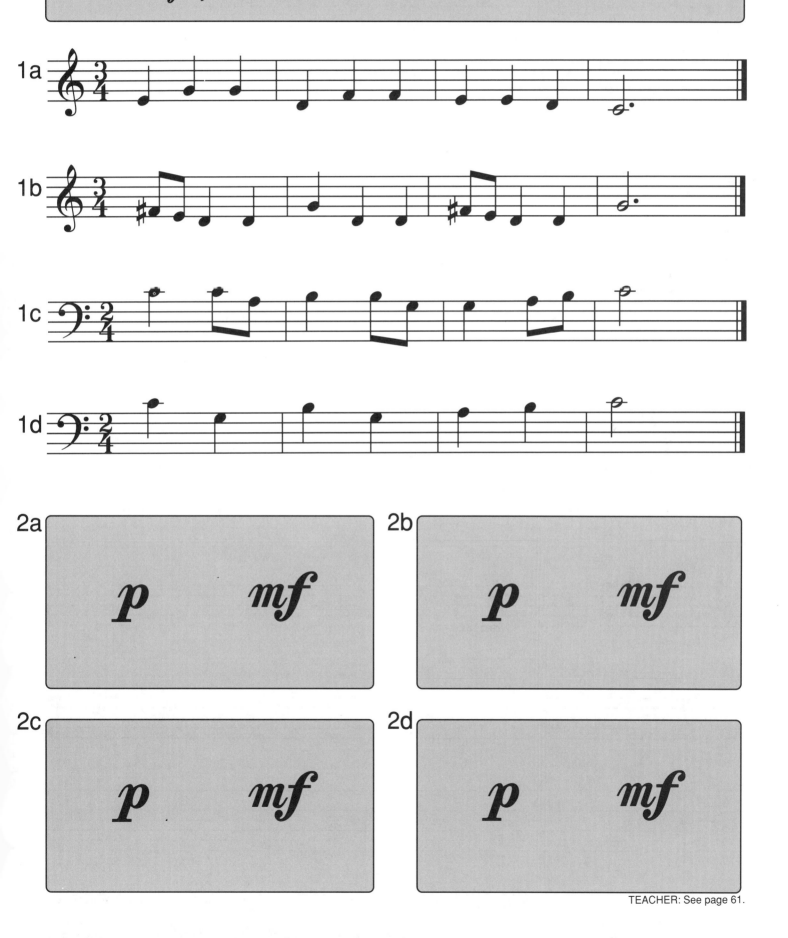

Use with page 50.

Eighth Notes

1. Your teacher will clap a rhythm pattern.
   Draw the missing note(s) in the box using ♩ or ♫

2. Your teacher will play four melodies. Each melody contains one ACCENT.

   Add an ACCENT SIGN under (♩) or over (♩) the note that is played LOUDER.
   　　　　　　　　　　　　 >

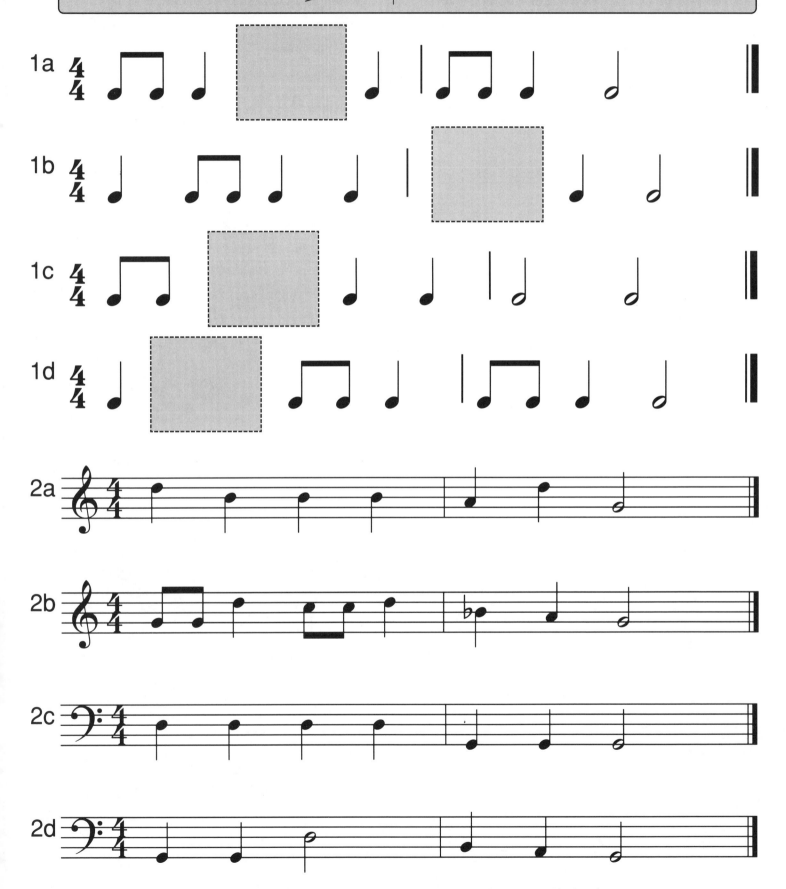

New G Position

1. Your teacher will play melodies in the NEW G POSITION.
   Draw the missing note(s) in the box.
2. Your teacher will clap a rhythm pattern.
   Circle the pattern that you hear.

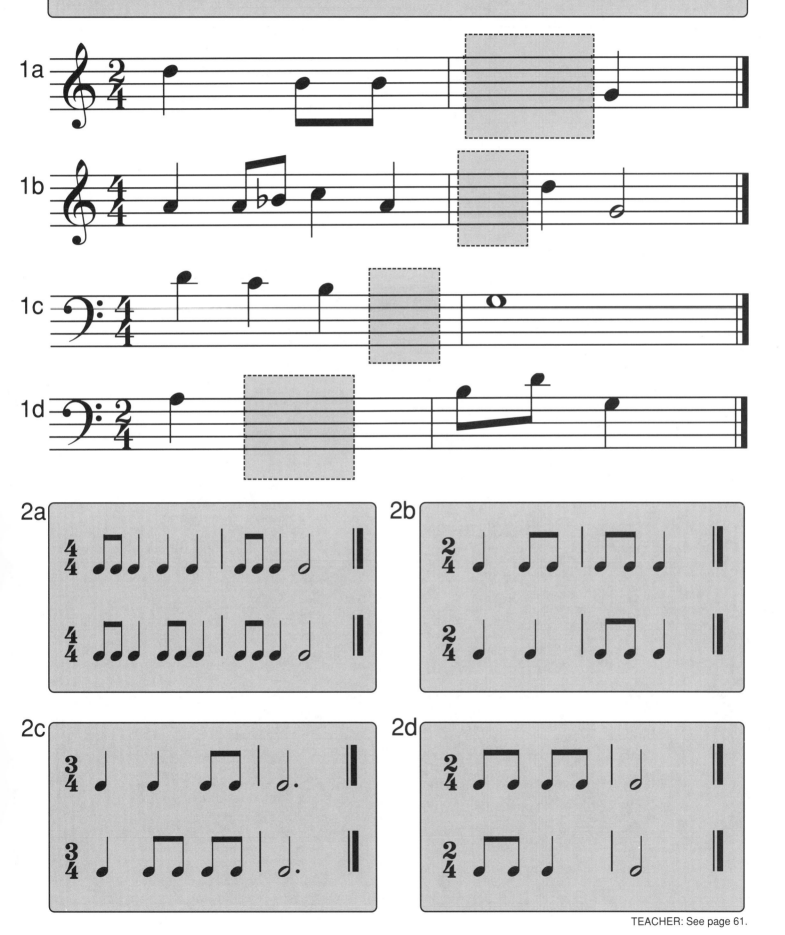

TEACHER: See page 61.

Use with page 52.

The Damper Pedal

1. Your teacher will play four melodies.
   Draw a PEDAL SIGN (⌐_____⌐) under the entire melody if the DAMPER PEDAL is used.
2. Your teacher will play MELODIC intervals of a 2nd, 3rd, 4th or 5th *above* the given note.
   • Draw the second note on the staff using a half note.
   • Write the interval number (2, 3, 4 or 5) on the line.

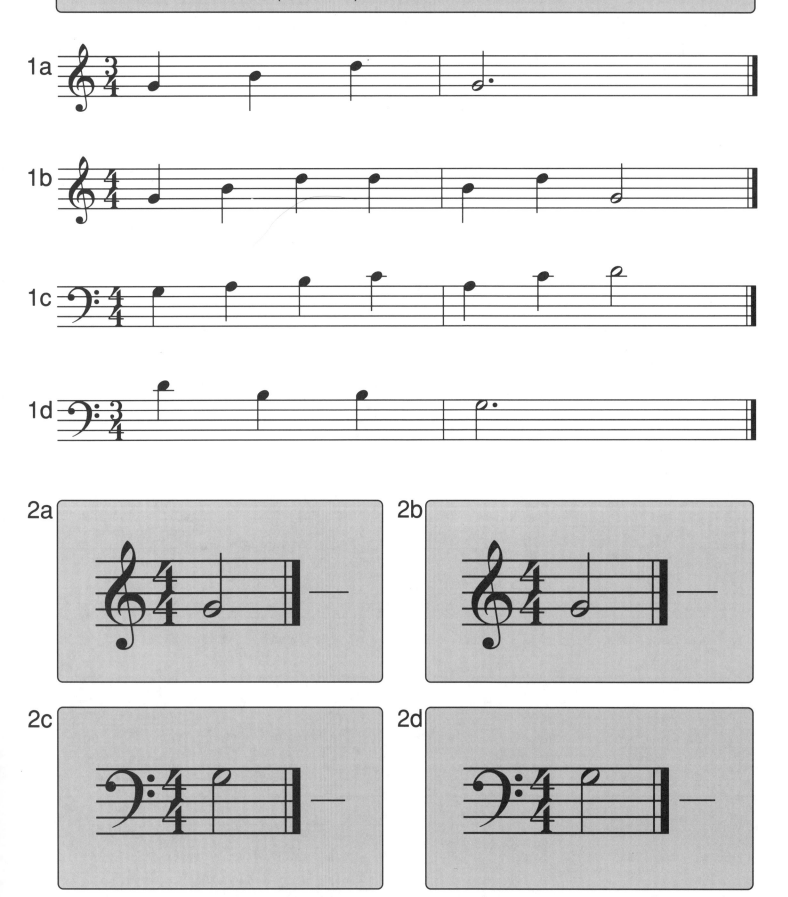

8va

1. Your teacher will play two notes.
   Write 8va above the second note if it is played one octave (8 notes) HIGHER than written.
2. Your teacher will play four melodies. Add an 8va sign (*8va - - ┐*) above the notes that are played one octave HIGHER than written.

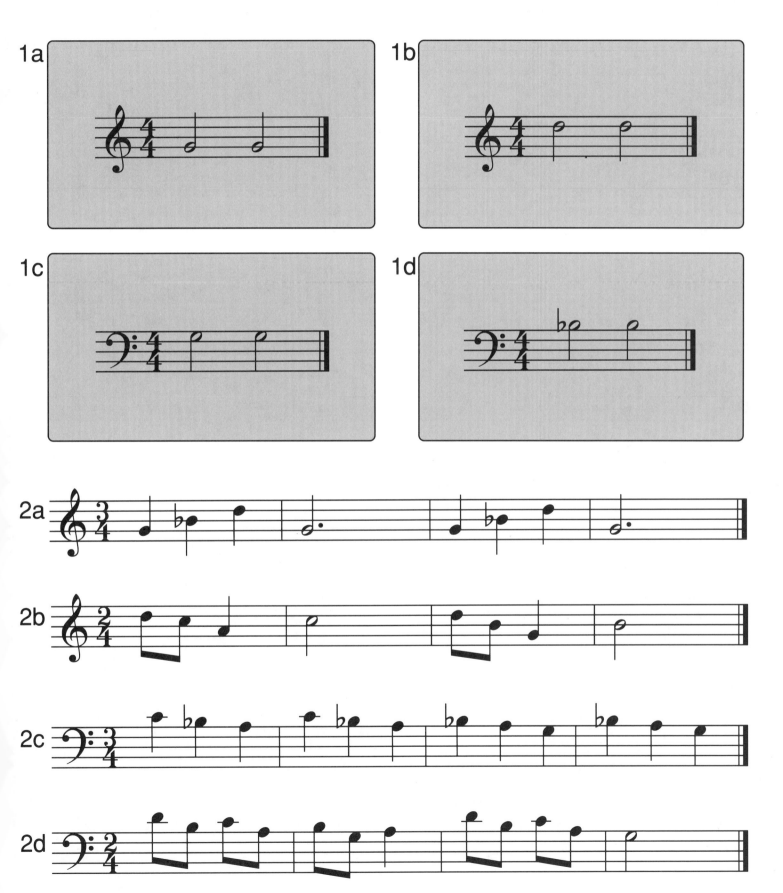

Use with pages 56–57.

Eighth Rest

1. Your teacher will clap a rhythm pattern. Circle the pattern that you hear.
2. Your teacher will play MELODIC or HARMONIC 2nds, 3rds, 4ths or 5ths.
   - Circle the example that you hear.
   - Write M if it is MELODIC or H if it is HARMONIC along with the interval number (2, 3, 4 or 5) on the line. Example: M2

1a
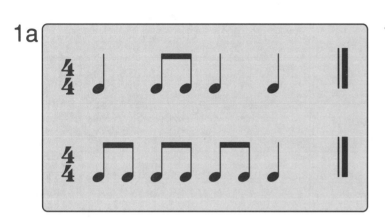

1b

1c

1d

2a

2b

2c
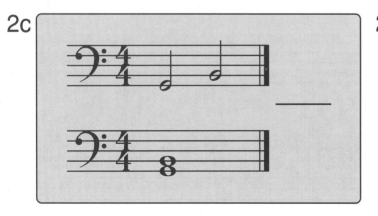

2d
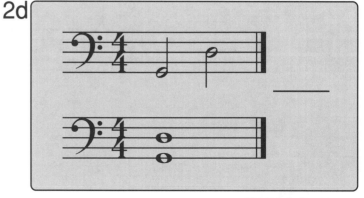

TEACHER: See page 62.

Middle D Position

1. Your teacher will play melodies in the MIDDLE D POSITION.
   One note in each melody will be played incorrectly. Circle the incorrect note.

2. Your teacher will play four melodies. Each melody contains one FERMATA.
   Add a FERMATA (𝄐) over the note that is held longer than its value.

Use with page 61.

Half Steps

1. Your teacher will play a HALF STEP that moves UP or DOWN.
   - If the second note moves UP a HALF STEP, draw a SHARP (♯) in front of it.
   - If the second note moves DOWN a HALF STEP, draw a FLAT (♭) in front of it.

2. Your teacher will play melodies containing HALF STEPS. Circle the melody that you hear.

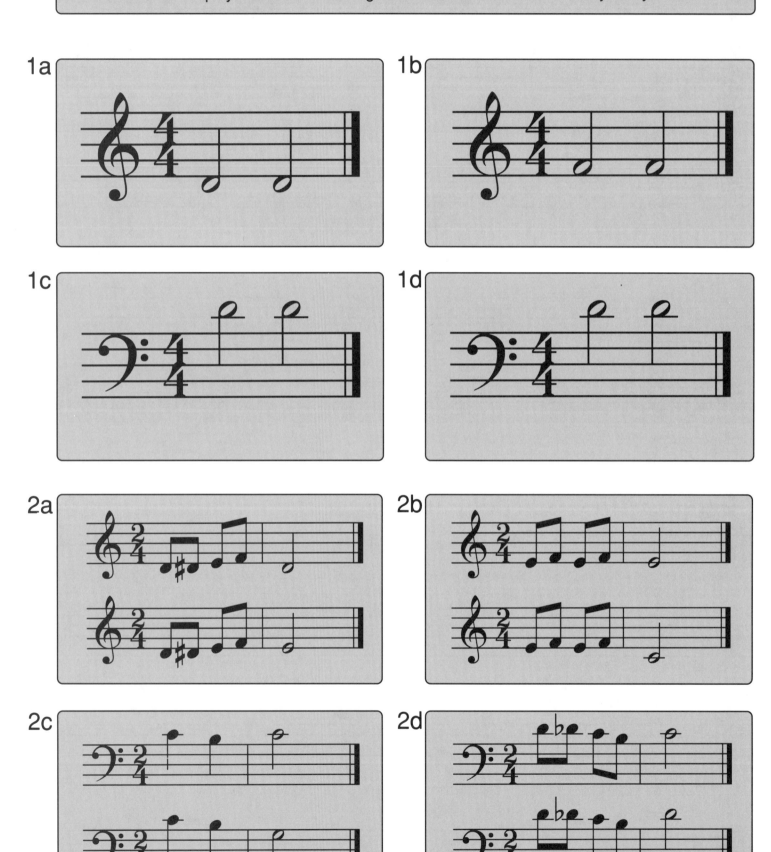

Whole Steps

1. Your teacher will play a WHOLE STEP that moves UP or DOWN.
   Draw the second note on the staff using a half note.
2. Your teacher will play melodies containing WHOLE STEPS.
   Circle the melody that you hear.

1a

1b

1c

1d
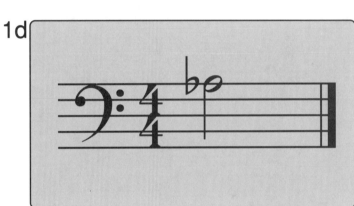

2a

2b
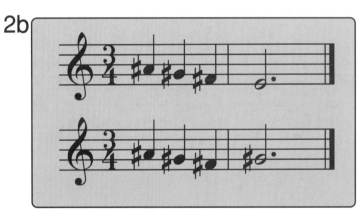

2c

2d
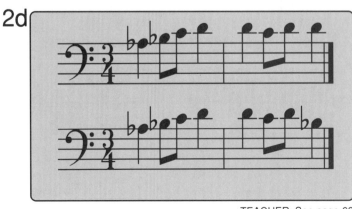

TEACHER: See page 63.

Use with page 64.

Tetrachords

1. Your teacher will play a HALF STEP or a WHOLE STEP.
   Circle the example that you hear.
2. Your teacher will play four-note TETRACHORD patterns.
   Draw the missing note in the box.

1a

1b

1c

1d

2a
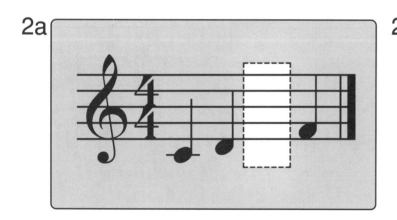

2b

2c
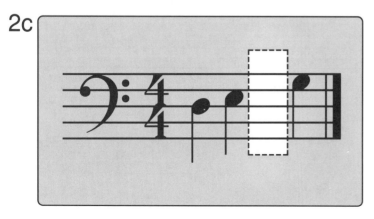

2d
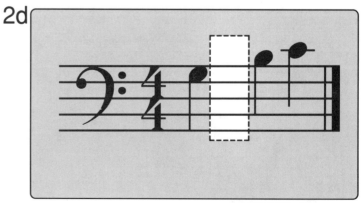

TEACHER: See page 63.

The Major Scale

1. Your teacher will play MAJOR SCALES. One note in each scale will be played incorrectly. Circle the incorrect note.
2. Your teacher will play MAJOR SCALES. Circle the rhythm pattern that you hear for each scale.

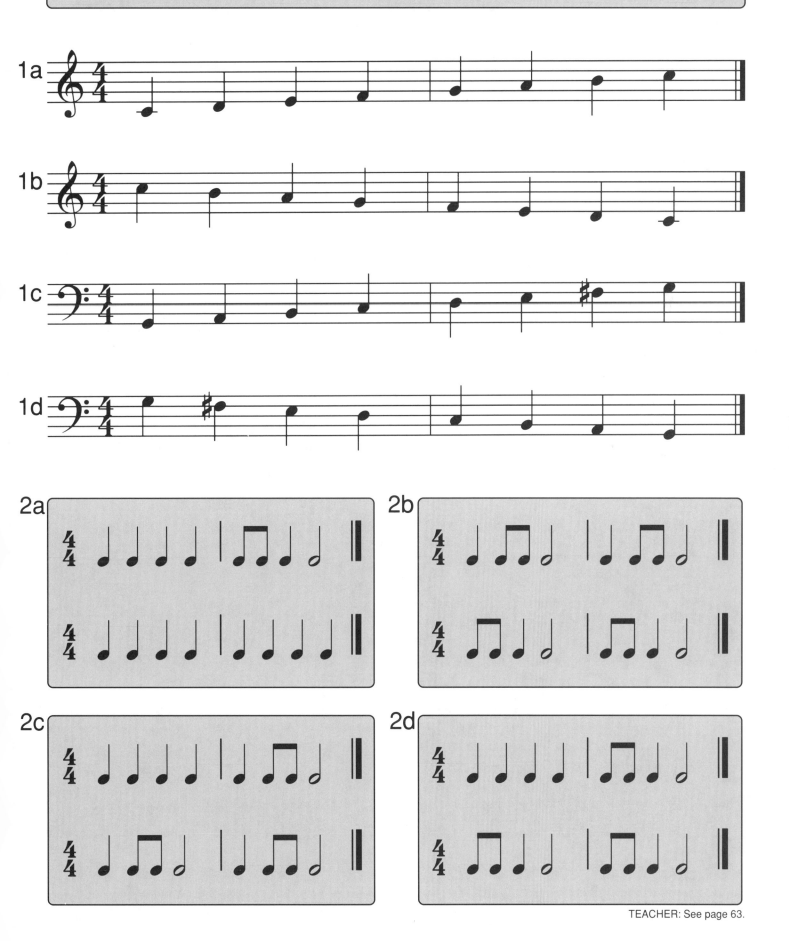

TEACHER: See page 63.

48

Use with page 66.

Key of G Major

1. Your teacher will play four melodies in the KEY OF G MAJOR.
   Draw the missing note in the box.
2. Your teacher will clap a rhythm pattern.
   Draw the missing notes and rests in the third measure, using ♩ ♫ ♩ ♩. and 𝄽

Use with page 67.

Intervals

1. Your teacher will play groups of HARMONIC intervals.
   Circle the group of intervals that you hear.
2. Your teacher will play four-note TETRACHORD patterns.
   Draw the missing note in the box.

1a

1b

1c

1d
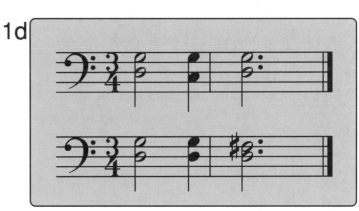

2a

2b
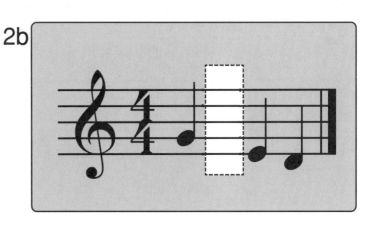

2c
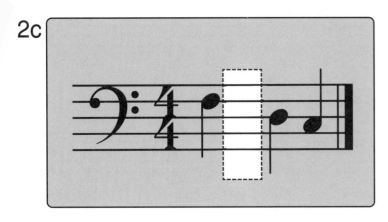

2d
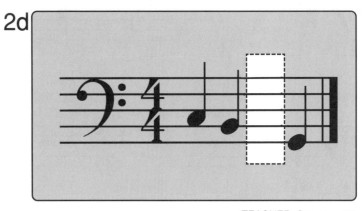

TEACHER: See page 64.

Use with pages 68–69.

Review

1. Your teacher will play a melody in $\frac{2}{4}$ or $\frac{3}{4}$ time.

   • Circle $\frac{2}{4}$ if you hear two beats in each measure.

   • Circle $\frac{3}{4}$ if you hear three beats in each measure.

2. Your teacher will play a two-note pattern. Circle the pattern that you hear.

3. Your teacher will play a melody in the G POSITION. Draw the missing note in the box.

4. Your teacher will play a melody that contains one ACCENT.
   Add an ACCENT SIGN under ( ) or over ( ) the note that is played LOUDER.

5. Your teacher will play a melody that contains a FERMATA.
   Add a FERMATA ( ) over the note that is held longer than its value.

6. Your teacher will play a melody that contains a RITARDANDO. Add the RITARDANDO (rit.)
   below the staff when the tempo begins to GRADUALLY SLOW DOWN.

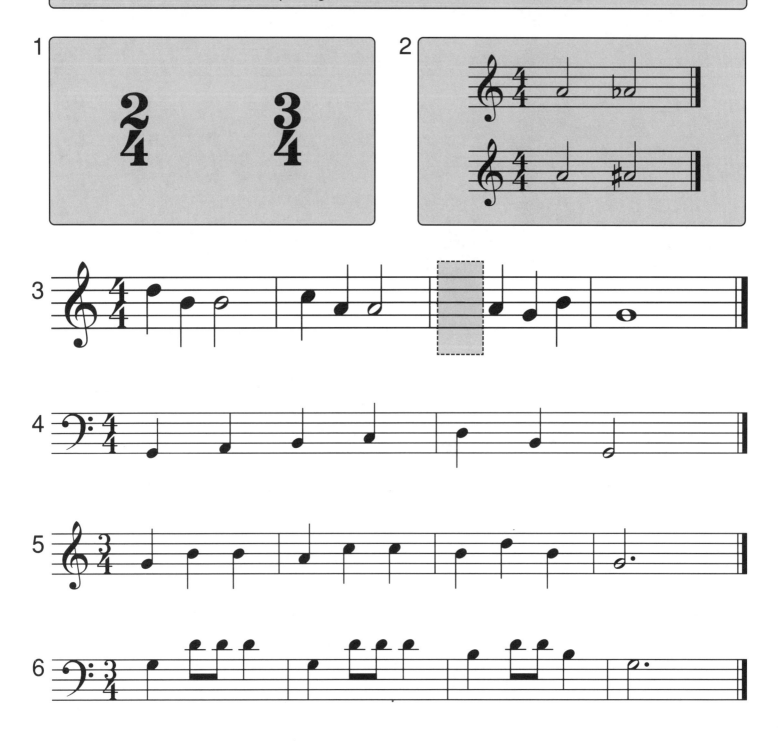

Review

1. Your teacher will play intervals of a 4th or 5th. Circle the interval that you hear.

2. Your teacher will play a HALF STEP or a WHOLE STEP. Circle the example (half or whole) that you hear.

3. Your teacher will clap a rhythm pattern. Complete the second measure using ♩ ♫ or ♩

4. Your teacher will play a melody. Draw a pedal sign (└────┘) under the entire melody if the DAMPER PEDAL is used.

5. Your teacher will play two notes. Write *8va* above the second note if it is played one octave HIGHER than written.

6. Your teacher will play a G MAJOR SCALE. One note will be played incorrectly. Circle that note.

TEACHER: See page 64.

Teacher's Examples

Page 3 (Play)

Page 4 (Clap)

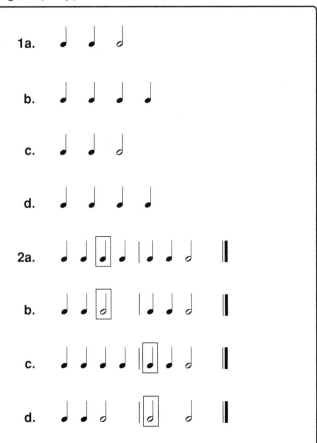

Page 5 (Clap)

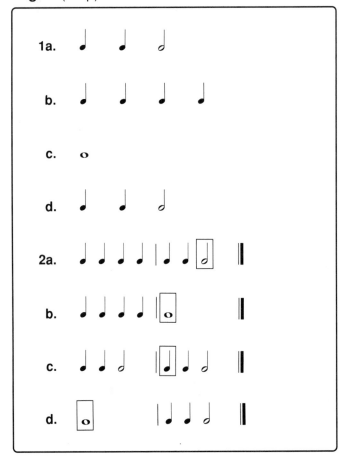

Teacher's Examples

Page 6 (Clap)

1a.

b.

c.

d.

2a.

b.

c.

d.

Page 7 (Play)

a.

b.

c.

d.

e.

f.

g.

h.

Page 8 (Play)

a.

b.

c.

d.

e.

f.

g.

h.

54

Teacher's Examples

Page 9 (Play)

Page 10 (Play)

Page 11 (Play)

Page 12 (Play)

Teacher's Examples

Page 13 (Clap)

Page 14 (Play)

Page 15 (Play)

Page 16 (Play)

Teacher's Examples

Page 17 (Clap)

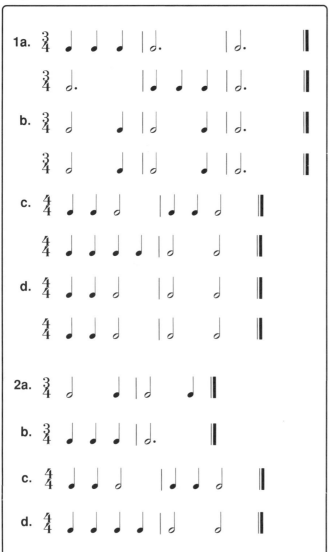

Page 18 (Play)

Page 19 (Clap)

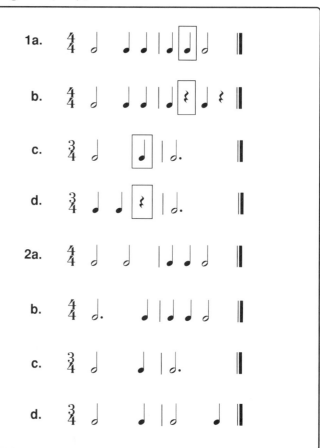

Page 20 (Play)

Teacher's Examples

Page 21 (Play)

Page 22 (Clap)

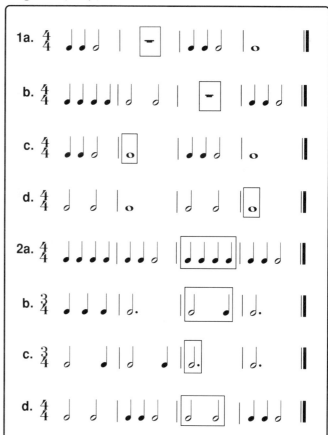

Page 23 (Play)

Page 24 (Play)

58

Teacher's Examples

Page 25 (Clap)

Page 27 (Play)

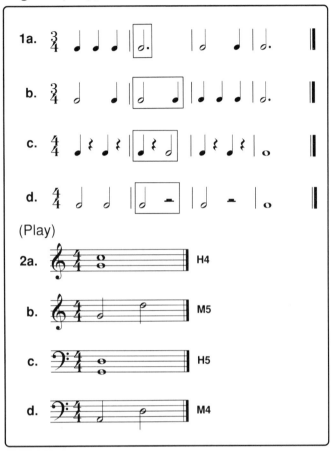

Page 26 (Play)

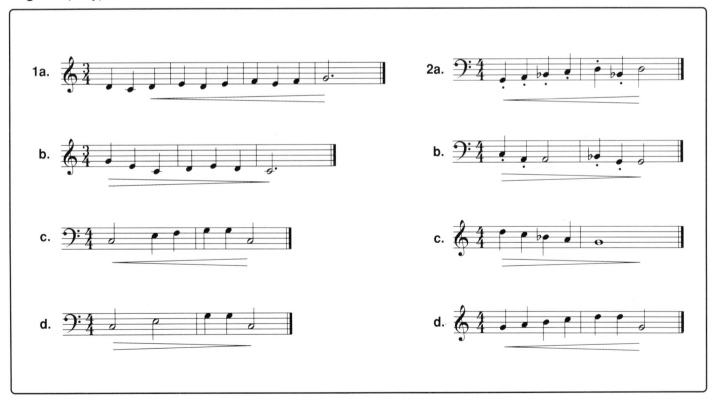

59

Teacher's Examples

Page 28 (Play)

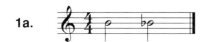

Page 29 (Play)

Page 30 (Play)

Page 31 (Play)

Teacher's Examples

Page 32 (Play)

Page 33 (Clap)

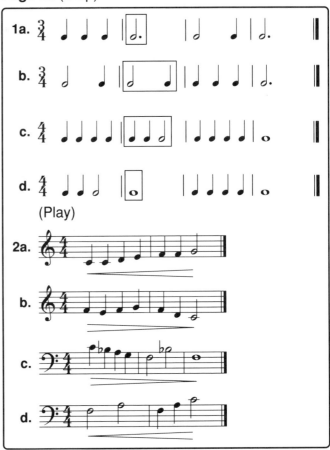

Page 34 (Play)

Page 35 (Clap)

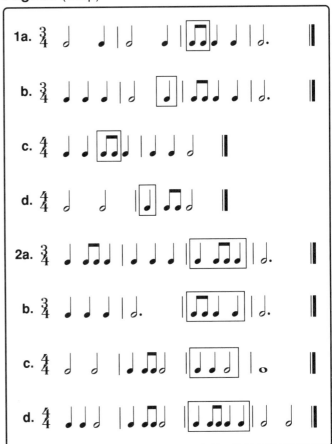

Teacher's Examples

Page 36 (Play)

Page 37 (Play)

Page 38 (Clap)

Page 39 (Play)

Teacher's Examples

Page 40 (Play)

1a.

b.

c.

d.

2a.   **5**

b.   **2**

c.   **3**

d.   **4**

Page 41 (Play)

1a.

b.

c.

d.

2a.

b.

c.

d.

Page 42 (Clap)

1a.

b.

c.

d.

(Play)

2a.   **H4**

b.   **M2**

c.   **H3**

d.   **M5**

Page 43 (Play)

1a.

b.

c.

d.

2a.

b.

c.

d.

Teacher's Examples

Page 44 (Play)

Page 45 (Play)

Page 46 (Play)

Page 47 (Play)

64

Teacher's Examples

Page 48 (Play)

Page 49 (Play)

Page 50 (Play)

Page 51 (Play)